Reliquary of Debt

Reliquary of Debt

Wendy Vardaman

ISBN: 978-1-943170-03-6

Cover Art: Erika Hibbert, "Scattered Reliquary" 2011
Cover Design: Wendy Vardaman
Interior Design: Bonnie Boyd
Production Director: Jane L. Carman

Typefaces: Garamond and American Typewriter

Published by: Lit Fest Press, Carman, 688 Knox Road 900 North, Gilson, Illinois 61436

festivalwriter.org

Acknowledgments

Thanks to the editors of the following journals and anthologies, which have published, sometimes under different titles, versions of these poems:

Antiphon: "(Florence. Santa Felicita. 10/8/2008)" *Assisi Journal*: "(Madison. Reliquary. St. Monica's Day)"
Cider Press Review: "(Sesto. Art History Lecture. 10/7/2008)"
Saint Peter's B-List, Contemporary Poems About the Saints (Ave Maria Press): "(Rome. Santa Marie en Cosmedin. 11/14/2008)"
Nerve Cowboy: "(Venice. Circling. 9/20/2008)"
qarrtsiluni: "(St. Joseph of Cupertino. 9/18/2008)," "(Arezzo. Casa Petrarch. 12/5/2008)"
Rosebud: "(Rome. Villa Borghese. 11/15/2008)"
ShepherdExpress: "(Rome. Santa Marie en Cosmedin. 11/14/2008)"
Slippage: "*Tortelli di Zucca Mantovani*"
Truck: "Postscript: *Post-colonial* pilgrims," "*Tortelli di Zucca Mantovani*"
Wisconsin Poets' Calendar: "Postscript: *Post-colonial* pilgrims"

This book began when my husband's job brought our family to Sesto Fiorentino, Italy, for a semester in a study-abroad program that rented space from the Villa Corsi Salviati on Via Antonio Gramsci (an unlikely combination of names and economics possible only in Italy). Thanks to the staff there; to the other faculty, especially Sy and Jo Mauskopf, wise, generous guides to the *Imperishable Masterpiece* and truly a second family to us; to the Livorni-Messina family for getting there before us and sharing their knowledge of the program; to our children for putting up with my frenetic attempts to pack two decades of deferred searching into four months and for leading from behind; and to the three of them, Conor, Greer, and Brendan, and my husband Thomas DuBois for countless creative conversations, laughter, and ideas. Greer is also co-creator of a larger project from which "GiottO : Jesture : Sleights of Hand : Arena Chapel" emerges; the form and the parts written by me included in this book would not exist without her, our conversations, and our larger collaboration. She was also the Latin expert on the other end of the "[Skype]" poems as well as a help with research and translation of material for "*Tortelli di Zucca Mantovani*," a poem written at the request of Madison Arts Commission to give its sister city Mantova, Italy, in 2013.

Many editor-writer-friends have read drafts of my work over the years, offering guidance and support. In addition to my family, thanks especially to Sarah Busse, Jane L. Carman, Martha Kaplan, and Margaret Rozga for believing in my poetry (or whatever it is) and not asking it to be something else. And thanks as always to my mother Lorna Vardaman whose belief is unshakeable.

For guides & traveling companions & all those who challenge us to find better paths.

Table of Contents

reliquary /ˈrɛlɪkwəɹi/

Etymology: From Middle French *reliquaire* (modern French *reliquaire*), from Late Latin *reliquiarium*, from *reliquia* ("a relic") (English *relic*), noun use of *reliquus* ("abandoned, left behind, relict"), from *relinquo* ("I relinquish"), from re- ("again") and *linquo* ("I leave, quit, forsake, depart from"), from Proto-Indo-European **leykʷ-* (cf. loan). (*Wiktionary*)

Postscript: *Post-colonial* pilgrims
November 2011

We were driving our children
crazy, but we didn't
know it, making them follow our wet
footsteps to approximately 111
churches in Italy. Where you swooned over finger bones, tongues, torn
cloak scraps, uncorrupted corpses. Where I fixed
my worship-wanting eyes on mud mixed
with marble. On chiseled lats & traps. On skin

& muscle modeled thick over thin, dark & light. They
were too polite to say what they believed.
That they'd seen enough. That it all looked
the same after the first seventeen or so.
That they wanted to eat, to relax. That they never got to lead.
That we were wearing them *out* & *through* with our lack.

Tortelli di Zucca Mantovani
    for Mantova, Italy, May 1, 2013

    Atreus Caecilius cucurbitarum/Sic illas quasi filios Thyestae/In
    partes lacerat secatque mille.—Martial, 1ˢᵗ C. CE

Cross breeder, easy mixer, *monoecious*—male and female flower on the same stem:
bees travel 15 kilometers with their messages, circling *zucca* to pumpkin,
no botanical obstacle or cultural barrier to mating *cucurbits*
of every shape, size, texture, color, which—wild or not—will resist disease, pest,
    drought.
When Martial called Caecilius *the Atreus of pumpkin*, he might have meant melon,
    meant

Lagenaria siceraria —gourd, vessel, container that traveled 10,000
years ago, Africa to the Americas; did not mean *zucca*, mean Mantovan
Piacentina, Marina di Chioggia, Americana, Turbante, whose oldest
seeds, like all cultivated *cucurbits*, are rooted in Oaxaca, Mexico,
8000 year-old *ayote* turned *askutasquash, pompion, pumpkin, zucca.*

Madison's pumpkins—large, round, bright orange—don't look like *zucca Mantovani*,
    what we
might call *squash*—Hubbard, Acorn, Festival, Delicata—making *gnocchi, risotto,*
tortelli, not *pie*, and the colors of Mantovan pumpkins run terra cotta
and *sinopia* to olive tree leaf and rosemary green, to mottled wall of pocked
palazzo; record ground, record quake, earth connected to earth—fractured plaster
    split

inviting us through and in between, like lines on pumpkin, stretch marks of ripening.
To go to Mantova directly, you must travel via these cracks widening
in aging fresco through *intonaco, arriccio*, garden clay. At the *Palazzo*

Ducale, where Montegna first painted the family Gonzaga as *real*, not allegory,
angels lean into their elbows on heaven's balcony, try to get a better view,

no way down from those illusionistic domes except by vine. In 1514,
Isabella d'Este Gonzaga, said to have *inspired tortelli di zucca*, went to Rome,
to *Villa Farnesina*, where the first painted *pumpkins* from the Americas
appeared three years after her visit and two centuries before any *botanical*
illustration. Perhaps *she* brought their seeds, rare gift that bloomed in soil then in the
    walls'

festoons. I've made pumpkin ravioli for friends without knowing it's the specialty
of Mantova but didn't think *México* either. Could buy it *Made in Italy*
at the Monroe Street *Trader Joe's* in Madison, where food from Europe sometimes
    means
urbanity, sometimes excess, but that's not *tortelli di zucca* made at home
in spite of the fuss or fresh-rolled and sold at the corner *pastificio*. Come

Tutti i Santi Ognissanti, women of a certain age bring flowers and *lumere* to the dead
during *passegiatta*. Slow walk. Drip, drip of day after day turned centuries. Turned
later to *tortelli di zucca*, not thinking *origin* but salty *&* bitter, sweet
& sour, hoping to lure home the living and the dead, they set new roots, spread their
    leaves,
recipes passed mother to daughter for longer than any memory, like seeds.

[Skype]

[4/11/13 12:23:34 AM] Poet: well the pumpkins at this point involve, in no particular order, Guilio Romano, Isabella d'Este, the Villa Farnesina in Rome, Anne of Burgundy and her book of hours, Louis XII, pumpkin ravioli, aka tortelli di zucca, Columbus and why are there 3 varieties of new world pumpkins in a fresco painted in 1515 anyway, a marriage gone sour, a jealous duke, a fashion doll, and The Winter's Tale

[4/11/13 12:23:37 AM] Poet: among other things

[4/11/13 12:23:48 AM] Poet: including halloween & thanksgiving

[4/11/13 12:23:57 AM] Poet: Latino farmworkers

[4/11/13 12:24:06 AM] Poet: the origin of gourds

[4/11/13 12:24:28 AM] Poet: competitive pumpkin farming

[4/11/13 12:24:35 AM] Poet: and the colors of pumpkins

[4/11/13 12:25:03 AM] Poet: so yeah. I just need to boil down 25 pages of notes into a 20-30 line poem, and I'll be good

[4/11/13 12:25:08 AM] Poet: :)

[4/11/13 12:26:18 AM] Poet: getting a little obsessive on the research… which means I'm getting a little behind on everything else.

[4/11/13 12:27:26 AM] Poet: & what does shakespeare have against mantua, anyway?

giornate

> *People go bankrupt all the time. Companies do, too. But countries?*—Eric Pfanner, "Iceland is all but officially bankrupt," *International Herald Tribune* (10-9-2008)

(Florence. Bus #2. 9/11/2008)

When I lose my wallet, new velvet
leather nap in tact, four annual passes to Florence's
state museums inside, used once,
forty euro tucked
between them, first
cash withdrawal in Europe since arriving, and for that matter, since
more than 20 years ago during which visit the disappearance
of 200 dollars during the first week would have meant

irrecoverable disaster—a month's living
expenses in a time we couldn't afford the *Uffizi*
once, much less a membership twice for four—I
regret only one thing: being
too cheap to buy *gelato* at the end of this hot & dusty
day after finally returning to the museum it took this long to see.

(Pompeii. Scavi. 11/29/2008)

More spectacular than any description
I've read of it, an entire city
with ancient roads, bakeries, villae
and brothels lies before us, and because it's the end
of November & intermittent thunderstorms, we're miraculously alone,
minimum bother from locals who need to
sell us books, umbrellas, cappuccino on the way,
provide commentary, taxi us between the ruin

and the train station. We fend them off with relative
ease, glimpse Vesuvius between storms that roll
through, eat salami & tomato sandwiches on the remains
of a Greek temple, and as the sun comes out to sink, arrive
at the forum, surrounded on all
four sides by public buildings whose form and function we still can recognize.

(Stratford-upon-Avon. New House. 10/21/2008)

No house exists here anymore—
the last owner refused
to pay taxes in 1759 and leveled
it so that none would ever be owed again—the house that Shakespeare
built then lived in after his retirement from the London theater.
Only the foundation remains, archeological ruins excavated
and exposed, surrounded by a restored
Elizabethan garden, in which stands another

testimony to the home's first and last owners—planted by one,
cut down by the other who grew
tired of pilgrims arriving almost
daily at his door demanding to see the poet's mulberry. Nearby the ruin
of the house stands another huge, gnarled tree,
sprung they say from a shoot of vanished parent.

(Milan. Duomo. 10/29/2008)

544 steps to the rooftop
where we mingle among 3400
statues & I don't know how many crenellated
spires, not as much to see in the distance as up
close between low-hanging clouds & crowds & cranes hovering above the cityscape
like angles in a painting by Mondrian & I still feel mad
not to have visited Chartres yesterday after my husband,
who never passes a church without going inside, decides it's too much effort to
    schlep

there from Paris for one cathedral,
and I let myself get talked out
of going, following to Versailles where we move like cattle through
the palace, packed shoulder to shoulder, and that's why, when he puts one careful
foot in front of the other here on the roof's ridge & I realize how far back he's
    dropped,
I don't slow down even though it's our birthday—

(Stratford-upon-Avon. The Birthplace. 10/21/2008)

I linger looking at the pane of window glass
now displayed under another layer
of glass, entire
sash intact, and etched into its surface,
pen-knifed names of poets who once
arrived to their saint's shrine. Picture
Coleridge, Wordsworth, Keats here,
unable to resist

the urge to leave some lasting mark.
I feel it, too, but can't
scratch my signature alongside. That's over.
Descend the stairs to sign the guestbook's
next blank line in ballpoint
on what I hope, at least, proves acid-free paper.

(Madison. Monroe St. 8/20/2008)

Though I hesitate to buy a day-old
muffin for a dollar at the coffee
shop, I'm simultaneously
researching the cost of travel
from Florence, where we'll live—husband's job—this fall,
to other parts of Europe. The children mock me.
Florence is close to Milan, which is on the way
to Paris, just a couple of hours from London, and Stratford-upon-Avon, almost

to Scotland. Before you know it, mock-me's booked
us on an Arctic cruise and a visit with the Inuit
via the Shetlands, Orkneys, and outer Hebrides. And my husband,
the Constant Traveler, confirms: *When we spent*
a year in Scandinavia, she wanted to get
to Italy. Now we're going to Italy, she plans to see England.

(London. Wyndham's Theater. 10/18/2008)

I can't get tickets for the RSC
Hamlet or even *Love's Labors Lost*
but manage to catch
Kenneth Branaugh in Tom Stoppard's new
translation of *Ivanov*. My son, who named his cat Vanya
two year's back, is just as glad to see Checkov
over Shakespeare, and my daughter gets over the embarrassment
of going to a famous actor's play

when it turns out to be good. The three of us spend
the afternoon laughing right up to the end
of each act—the bloody nose Chekov wanted
to give his audience after making them howl, and when
it's over, I resist the desire to line up at the backstage door—tuck my program inside
my bag instead, head to the National Portrait Gallery to crush on the dead.

(Milan. Santa Marie de Grazie. 10/29/2008)

It occurs to me, minutes into my quarter
hour before Leonardo's not-so-faded
fresco in Milan, studying the angles of inclined
heads, of hands, and beginning to piece together,
as I budget time, the relations among his onlookers, to wonder
what, exactly, the guard whose job entails watching me watch this painted
image of Christ handing out bread
to disciples at the Last Supper

can possibly do with herself all
day, trapped in this dim cell, bare but for a few benches, her straight
backed chair and two frescoes—one, the world's most well-known,
the other unseen on the back wall,
a crucifixion scene we all plan to glance at on the way out,
which I turn toward now, attempt to take a Christian interest in.

(London. National Portrait Gallery. 10/18/2008)

Passing Shakespeare,
hanging lonely at the end of an aisle
of Tudors who line the walls, I smile
to myself, at him, color
up like a love-struck teen with a major
crush, keep finding, while my kids look on, excuses to stroll
this way again, trying to act casual,
like I hardly even notice *him*, over there,

desperate for one more sidewise glimpse,
a fast last look, one word, a nod—
point us like needles to the center through which all loops thread,
ignoring as I make my fifth or sixth
fool's pass the kids' attempts to turn me toward
some other, unexhausted end.

(Sesto. Via Gramsci. St. Joseph of Cupertino's Day)

Maybe it's the light head, wanting
in mental capacity, so that when Joseph studies
for a test, he focuses on one item only. Prays
for his examiners to ask that question. Flying,
however, comes easily, happens trancing
on God, involuntary. One minute he's
with his fellow Franciscans, the next he's taken off. It happens
first on the order's feast day, then with increasing

frequency. He can't stop, poor empty-
handed priest, no matter the ascending rank of those who order
him not to make a spectacle of himself.
Exiled by the pope to Assisi then to one commune and the next, he goes dry—
ordered not to speak to anyone other
than his bishop—until the last mass, Assumption Day, overcome by happiness, he
    lifts off.

(London. King's Cross. 10/24/2008)

Even my fifteen-year-old wants to see
it, I discover, after making a useless
circuit through the station, looking for the entrance
to the wizard world. *Do you want to go
back?* I ask, but they won't admit they do,
embarrassed by this bit of childishness,
so in the end I have to insist.
It won't take long. When would we

ever be anywhere this close again? And so we take
one more careful lap and find ourselves at last,
porters rushing past, across from *Platform 9 ¾* where my daughter
snaps one quick shot, no one else midweek
to jostle us, a long way off again when the disappointed son reveals he hasn't
seen the sign, didn't even notice we were there.

(Sesto. Ginori Porcelain Factory. 12/12/2008)

Museum of china plates, painted
with flowers that bloom on hill
tops above town, spill
over with mismatched Italian scenes—Venetian canals, ruined
Pompeii, Rome's forum looking three hundred
years ago much as it did last week, with some additional
tableaux of goddesses in pastoral
settings, shepherds who woo them with unceasing serenade

in praise of their beauty, bounty, wit, etc., while all around
sit plastic buckets spread to catch
the quickest leaks, ceiling dripping
end to end,
puddles collecting beside long glass
cases that prevent idle shepherds and their idylls from a soaking.

(Madison. Reliquary. St. Monica's Day)

Half-way tempted minutes after you leave
to sweep up the trimmings from your last
haircut
off the bathroom floor, the sink, the countertop, and save
them in some sacred box—the way I've saved
each lost tooth, last
bits of blood still clinging to their worn roots—
I brush my hand across fogged glass, remove

the curled lock pasted there, scrap-booked valentine,
yellow-edged, from someone who no longer calls,
transport this last
of you that's left on the end of one
processional fingertip, careful not to let it drop until
I reach its final resting place—the trash.

(Florence. Hotel Cimabue. 10/13/2008)

He's not a little boy, the boy
in the lobby leaning
against his father's chest and whimpering
softly as the man explains the problem at the desk. Lucky
for him she speaks perfect English, and he doesn't have to use his few
Italian phrases involving *doctor, clinic, accident*, while the boy, bleeding
through bandages wrapping
his hand cries harder. His father wants to know

how far to the nearest After-Hours
Clinic, can they walk there or could she call
a taxi, while she explains in clear, measured
sentences, twice, as if speaking to a child, that of course
the doctor will come late on a Sunday evening to the hotel,
no extra charge. *Please, go back to the room, lie down, apply pressure to the wound.*

[Skype]

[4/20/13 4:20:51 PM] Poet: trying to sort all my pumpkin, mantua, etc. research …

[4/20/13 4:21:07 PM] Poet: I keep thinking, "why did I find this interesting?"

[4/20/13 4:21:12 PM] Poet: :)

[4/20/13 4:21:31 PM] Poet: difference between poet/scholar

[4/20/13 4:21:48 PM] Poet: unable to sustain long term fascination with trivial details

[4/20/13 4:21:54 PM] Poet: as opposed to short term

[4/20/13 4:23:43 PM] Poet: I did find out yesterday that the Villa Farnesina builder/ owner wanted to marry the illegitimate daughter of Francesco Gonzaga (Isabella d'Este's husband) which is how I now theorize that the pumpkin seeds went from his garden to them

[4/20/13 4:24:11 PM] Poet: in direct fashion …

[4/20/13 4:24:22 PM] Poet: but then again, it could have been from them to him

[4/20/13 4:24:36 PM] Poet: they could have had them first

[4/20/13 4:24:53 PM] Poet: & he's just the one with the paintings

from *Mantova, Italy*, a Wikiprosepoem

Make additions & corrections. Last updated |*date*|. Some references needed.

Anselm of Lucca, the Younger

Patron saint of Mantova, feast day March 18. Named bishop of Lucca by his uncle/ pope. Resigned. Became a monk. Devoted to quiet, to contemplation. No miracles as far as anyone records except repeated refusal to indulge himself, be vested with worldly power, take advantage of family connections. Keeps tourism at low levels in Mantova as well as in Lucca, cf. Shakespeare.

Coffee

Caffe Borsa Mantova Pasticceria Antoniazzi Caffe Libenter Bar Venezia Bar Posta Bar Hemingway Café Bar Sossi Bar Antonella Bar Noce di Romanelli Alfredo Bar Penny Black Tabaccheria Bar Sordello Bar Cin Cin Bar Roxy Bar Irish di Scalari Gianfranco Bar Wall Street di Hu Maria Baby Bar Break Bar di Penitenti Katia Caffe Quadrifoglio di Hu Yinguang Angels' Bar Bar Virgilio Petit Café Ag Bike and Coffee.

Cracks

To travel to Mantova directly, you must go via cracks widening in the frescoes, through *intonaco* and *arriccio*, at the *Palazzo Ducale*. In the *Camera degli Sposa* where Montegna painted the ducal family, dog, servants, furniture, angels lean over heaven's balcony trying to get a better view, though it isn't likely from those illusionistic heights. This is before the introduction of *Curcubita maxima* to Mantova, and there is no way down.

Tourists come through, 5 minutes per group. The guard, not allowed to read, to text, to listen to music, sits in a folding chair, knows every wrinkle on the faces of the duke and duchess, those that were painted and those that weren't. This is not an allegory, but it is a metaphor.

Di Zucca in Zucca

Festival of *zucca* held mid-September-early December. One of numerous celebrations in Mantova, including the *Festivaletteratura*. Cross-pollination of these two events might result in poems carved on illuminated pumpkins & poetic recipes for *Tortelli di zucca* from every local fictional character, cf. *Virgil's Pumpkin Ravioli, Squash Risotto Romeo, Torta di zucca Isabella <3 Giulio, Palla di zucca di Rigoletto, Zuppa di zucca Atreus*, etc.

Festa di Tutti i Santi

Holy Day of Obligation. Women of a certain age put on fur regardless of heat, carry flowers to graves, cf. *passegiatta*, steady stream flowing through the streets and into cemeteries lined with *lumere*.

Isabella d'Este Gonzaga (1474-1539)

Admired by Anne de Bretagne, who kept a fashion doll of Isabella. Anne's husband, Louis XII of France, had a diplomatic encounter with Isabella in 1500. The very first image of *Cucurbit* (pumpkin/squash) from the Americas appears in *Grandes Heures d'Anne de Bretagne*, c. 1505, and predates the more botanically accurate images at the *Villa Farnesina* by a decade. Isabella wrote thousands of surviving letters, currently in process of digitization. A project that visualizes Isabella's 16th c. *social network* is underway. Founded a school for girls in Mantova. Favorite food said to be *Tortelli di Zucca*.

Married to Francesco II Gonzaga, duke of Mantua and Captain General of the Venetian armies, who periodically went missing in wars, affairs and syphilitic insanity, leaving Isabella to raise eight children and defend Mantua in his various absences, which she did.

The scholarly poem *"Tortelli di Zucca Mantovani"* (2013) argues that Isabella received some of the first pumpkin seeds from the Americas by way of her cousin for whom she was named, Queen Isabella of Spain, then gifted them to her followers, including Anne of Bretagne and banker Agostino Chigi, who built the *Villa Farnesina*.

Flora di Mantova

This entry does not exist.

Fresco (cf. Muralism, Mexican)

Vehicles of cultural and scientific information, e.g., *Wedding Banquet of Cupid & Psyche*, Villa Farnesina (1515-18), which contains 170 types of flora, including three distinct varieties of *Cucurbits* (pumpkin) from the new world. An artscience laboratory. A maker-space.

Giornata (pl. Giornate)
A day's work, usually, in reference to *fresco*.

Gonzaga
Not to be confused with the American university located in Spokane, Washington.

Lago Pajolo
Created 1198 by Alberto Pitentio as part of the aquatic fortification, aka ring of lakes, of Mantova. Formed by redirection of the River Mincio. Gone missing. Dried up c. 18th c., though for all practical purposes, Mantova remains an island.

Librogusterini
Combines in a single Mantovan convenience store three necessary elements of life: books, cheese, coffee.

Mantova
Not to be confused with Mantua, Ohio; Mantua, Utah; Mantua, New Jersey; Mantua, Virginia; the Mantua district of Philadelphia, Pennsylvania; the village of Mantua in Baltimore County, Maryland; the hamlet of Mantua in Greene County, Alabama; and a location in Monroe County, Iowa.

Mantua Philadelphia
Site of Dupree Studios, artistic home of African-American painter and muralist James Dupree, whose three-year battle against the seizure of the studio through eminent domain has finally ended in his favor (Fall 2014). "Mr. Dupree has used his success as an artist to reinvest in the Philadelphia communities of his roots. There are many well-known examples of that investment, but one example that stands out is his studio in the Mantua neighborhood. His success is a product of the best Philadelphia art institutions, and he is an exemplary model of a Philadelphian investing back in his community. Part of his long term goals, his dream, has been to leave Dupree Studios as a pillar in the Mantua community"(*Save Dupree Studios*).

Mantus
From Etruscan *Arides Mantus*, aka *Hades*. Romans attributed *Mantus* etymologically to *Manto*, daughter of *Tiresias*, the blind nonbinary prophet & patron/(ess) of poets, falsely slandered along with Manto by Mantova's most famous literary citizen, Virgil, cf. Professional jealousy, Shakespeare.

Miracles
Cf. Anselm of Lucca, Shakespeare, Tiresias, *Tortelli di zucca*, pumpkin seeds, saving Dupree Studios.

Oaxaca, México
Location of oldest cultivated pumpkin seeds (8000-10,000 BCE).

Orange
In Renaissance Europe, an amusing color, associated with Bacchus, god of parties, drinks, festivals, feasting.

Palazzo Te
See *Sala dei Giganti*, see Romano, see *fresco*, see Gonzaga, see reed ceilings.

Painters of Isabella d'Este
Leonardo, Mantegna, Romano, Titian.

Passegiatta
Holistic expression of creative life force in Italian culture. To move the feet as well as the hands/the mouth. To gravitate toward friends/neighbors/family. To know stroll, amble, this slow way, drip of days become centuries, low scrub of olive trees always over the shoulder hillside.

Poems Set in Mantova
        (*This entry is a stub. Please add material.*)
Cf. *Divine Comedy* (portions), *Rigoletto*, *Romeo & Juliet*, *Taming of the Shrew*, *Tortelli di zucca Mantovani* (this entry cannot be verified and may be removed), *Two Gentleman of Verona*, *The Winter's Tale*.

Poets of Mantova
Cf. Constanzo Beschi, Isabella d'Este, Monteverdi, Shakespeare, Sordello, Virgil.

Pumpkin
American. Cross-breeder, *monoecious* (cf. Tiresias). From L. *pepo*, Fr. *pompion*, "to ripen." Not to be confused with its botanical twin *squash*, from *askutasquash* [Algonquin]. Mostly cultivated (and tasteless) *Cucurbita maxima*. In order to qualify for "largest pumpkin" contest, the *cucurbita* must be 80% orange and preferably round, despite the fact that other colors are botanically indistinguishable from the orange variety. Cleaned and arranged on straw, cf. *pumpkin patch*, pumpkins draw consumers from 30 miles (50 km) or more to *pick their own* during October in preparation for celebrating Halloween.

These pumpkins, which can also be purchased at nearby stores, are hollowed, carved, and set on porches. They deteriorate quickly. Uncarved pumpkins have significantly greater longevity. *Squash* preferred for consumption.

Once a desperation food commonly given to livestock, grown on plantations by e.g., Washington and Jefferson, the gigantic pumpkin (C. *maxima*), symbolizes in late 20th c. American harvest rituals *moral virtue, farm life, family gathering, rustic past*. Indigenous peoples throughout the Americas cultivated pumpkins prior to and following European contact, sown symbiotically with beans and corn. First appearance of *pumpkin pie* in an American cookbook, *American Cookery*, 1796, based on recipes in English and French cookbooks. Obvious racial component to the appearance of *pumpkin pie* as staple of *Thanksgiving*, created 1863, as a holiday to (re)establish American national identity around new world ingredients detached from indigenous foodways, cf. Nativism (not to be confused with Native American).

The *Starbucks pumpkin spice latte* contains no pumpkin. At Trader Joe's, you can purchase pumpkin ravioli *Made in Italy* (cf. *Tortelli di zucca*).

More than 2000 lbs. (900 kilo): the inedible winning pumpkins at the Ohio Valley Giant Pumpkin Growers' annual weigh-off at Canfield's Parks Garden Center.

Pumpkinification

Satirical deification of pumpkin. Cf. Falstaff in *The Merry Wives of Windsor*, *The Legend of Sleepy Hollow*. Traceable to the *Apocolocyntosis divi Claudii* (*Pumpkinification of the Divine Claudius*), although the *pumpkin* of Seneca, like those of Martial, would not have been the *Cucurbits* of Oaxaca or the Americas.

Pumpkin Seed

Now the only edible part of large *C. maxima*, toasted at home in ovens and eaten as part of *pumpkin carving* event, or purchased and consumed as *trail mix* or *Pumpkin-Spiced Pumpkin Seeds* (Trader Joe's). Note that oldest pumpkin seeds, 10,000–8000 BCE, have been found in Oaxaca, Mexico, and predate corn and beans by 4000 years. Appropriate gift for Renaissance rulers and aristocrats, small packets of seeds were mailed to important religious and political personages as soon as the first voyages returned from the Americas. Of course seeds of the pumpkin would have found their way into the hands of Isabella d'Este, namesake of her cousin, Queen Isabella of Spain.

Redirecting Rivers

Cf. *Mincio*, hydraulic engineering (renaissance), artificial lakes (four) of Mantova, *Sala dei Giganti*.

Reed Ceilings

Cf. *Lago Pajolo*, Bell Tower of the Palatine Basilica of Santa Barbara. Used to create more flexible structures in Renaissance buildings. Life limit of reeds does not exceed 500 years.

Giulio Romano

That rare Italian master. Fictional character in Shakespeare's early magical realist, late historical romance, *The Winter's Tale.* Created the statue called *Hermione.* Only named artist in Shakespeare's *oeuvre.* Died in Mantova.

Sala dei Giganti

Guilio Romano. Jupiter hurls the other gods from Mount Olympus. cf. Artistic envy, Giulio Romano, Virgil, Isabella d'Este, Redirecting rivers. Painted 1532–34, noted for illusionistic ceiling fresco, cf. Antonio da Corregio's cupola fresco of the Assumption, 1526–30, cf. verse drama. When giants come and go from Mount Olympus, they go by pumpkin vine.

Shakespeare

Semi-fictional character responsible for modern rebranding of Mantua, its signature ingredient, pumpkin, its foremost artist, Guilio Romano, and its most significant political/ agricultural/ social/ urban planning genius, Isabella d'Este (cf. Hermione).

Bartolomeo Stefani

Author of *L'Arte di Ben Cucinare*, 1662, chef to the Gonzagas, claimed by some as the source of first published recipe for *Tortelli di zucca*, though predated by "tortelli di zucca con il butirro" (pumpkin tortelli with butter), almost identical to contemporary preparation, in the cookbook *Dello Scalco* written by Giovan Battista Rossetti, cook in the court of Duke Alfonso II d'Este in Ferrara, and published in 1584. Duke Alfonso II d'Este was the grandson of Anne of Brittany and Louis XII of France, whom Isabella d'Este met in 1500 and persuaded not to invade Mantova, as well as Isabella's nephew, the son of her brother Alfonso I.

Table

A flat, possibly wooden surface, used to hold plates (multi-use food containers). Can be found at cafes, restaurants, private homes. Often surrounded by chairs. A place to sit down and eat, often shoulder to shoulder, with other people. Facilitates conversation and storytelling.

Teatro All'antica

Located in Sabbioneta, province of Mantua, on *Via Giulia.* One of only three surviving Renaissance theaters. The second-oldest surviving indoor theater in the world. The first free-standing building constructed 1588–90 (aka *lost years* of Shakespeare) as a theater. In the world.

Tortelli di Zucca

For the filling:
2 1/4 pounds (1 k) zucca
4 ounces (100 g) amaretti (almond macaroons)
4 ounces (100 g) mostarda
2 cups (100 g) grated Parmigiano
Salt
A little (1/8 teaspoon or so) freshly grated nutmeg
For the pasta:
3 cups (350 g) flour
2/3 cup (100 g) semolina
4 whole eggs
1 tablespoon milk
For the sauce:
2/3 cup unsalted butter, melted
2 cups freshly grated Parmigiano

Specialty of Mantova. Combining pumpkin (*zucca*), *amaretti*, *mostarda*—all local ingredients—in pasta. Served to the dead on All Saints' Eve, whose way, grave to table, is lit by *lumere*. What lures them back from where they lose the memory of themselves as other than earth for as long as possible. How this process took place before the invention of the recipe, which goes back to the table of Isabel d'Este, is unknown, though it may have had something to do with Tiresias and Virgil. Perhaps the dead remained in the earth. Perhaps they gathered over other foods in other homes.

You can try to make *Tortelli di zucca* at Elisabetta Arcari's cooking school, *Peccati di gola*, in a 14th century Mantovan Palazzo. It will not be easy. You can eat them at *Osteria delle Quattro Tette* [Vicolo Nazione 4, +39 03763 29478] at communal tables. You can try to make them at home. Say a prayer to Saint Anselm of Lucca, be patient, prepare to fail.

You must imagine, while you consume the signature dish of Mantova, Isabella d'Este Gonzaga, 1474–1539. Queen Elizabeth I was a six-year-old when Isabella died. The shapes of *Tortelli di zucca* are as varied as Isabella's: mother, wife, woman, aristocrat, trend-setter, political disciple of Machiavelli, musician, peace-maker, artist, writer, renaissance woman, student and leader of industry, of agriculture, educator of girls.

Drawn by Leonardo, painted by Mantegna, Romano, Titian, among others. Visited Rome and the *Villa Farnesina* in 1514. Feted by Agostino Chigi, banker & theatrical producer, at his newly built suburban home. Agostino hoped to marry Margherita Gonzaga, *natural daughter* of Francesco II Gonzaga, husband to Isabella d'Este, but it didn't work out.

Tortelli di Zucca Mantovani [Poem Text]
This entry has been removed.

Villa Farnesina
After Isabella d'Este's visit to Chigi's *Villa*, the first illustrations of cultivated pumpkins, *C. maxima*, *pepo*, *moschata*, appeared there among 170 botanically accurate images of fruits and vegetables in the festoons of the *Loggia di Amore e Psiche*, *Villa Farnesina*, Rome, 1515–18. These fresco images predate any scientific documentation of variation among or illustrations of new world *Cucurbit* by 250 years, the *first* European illustrations saving one, that in the *Grandes Heures d'Anne de Bretagne*, c. 1505, cf. Anne de Bretagne (Brittany), who kept a fashion doll of Isabella.

Giulio Romano was then an assistant in the workshop of Raphael, the frescoist of *Villa Farnesina*. Romano later became the frescoist of the *Palazzo Te* at the invitation of Isabella. He also painted Isabella.

Cucurbit may have been rapidly carried from the Americas by officials, such as Peter Marty D'Anghara, courtier and chaplain to Queen Isabella of Spain, gifting the powerful with seeds in letters, and/or by sailors and/or by diners at the tables of banker Agostino Chigi doing the same. But some of those *powerful* officials and letter writers would have been, e.g., Queen Isabella and her namesake, Isabella d'Este, known as one of the most prolific letter writers in 16th c. Europe.

The assumption, as in Janick and Paris 2006, that pumpkin seed traveled via male rather than female hands in all of the *scholarly* literature on its transmission is gender-biased on multiple levels, blind to the historical realities of female political power during the era, and a third-hand misapplication of the metaphor of *seed*—a problematic biological characterization (plant seeds not being at all *like* semen) further and inapplicably projected onto the politics of communication and gift giving. Stop and think about it for a minute: *seed givers* as *pumpkin* seed givers?

Picture Isabella removing the sealing wax from an envelope at her desk and carefully emptying ten or so of these seeds into her palm. Picture the giver: male and female, *monoecious*. Picture the pumpkins she birthed in her garden then shared with *her* circle, not to mention the food, the art, the ties between us *and* the metaphors: growth, mother, party, cultural travel, conversation, cultivation, curious, home, transformation, decay.

Virgil

A poet of Mantova. Professional jealousy of possibly responsible for Mantova's punning rebranding as *death* (cf. male *Mantus* [Hades] v. female *Manto*) by Shakespeare. (Mantua is mentioned exactly 14 times in *Romeo & Juliet*, the place of Romeo's exile: *And world's exile is death: then banished,/ Is death mis-term'd.*)

Zucca (Cucurbit)

> *There may be no other family of plants in which the misuse of names has been so widespread.... Hence, artistic detail and literary accuracy are of the utmost importance for enabling the correct identification of cucurbit taxa.—"The Cucurbits of Mediterranean Antiquity: Identification of Taxa from Ancient Images and Descriptions," Annals of Botany (2007)*

When Martial wrote *cucurbitarum*, 1st c. CE, he likely meant *Lagenaria siceria*, ancient container crop native to Zimbabwe. *Cucurbitarum* is a confusing term for Classical scholars, along with the related, *pumpkinification*. *Lagenaria* cultivated for food, medicine, containers, household goods, shade could, in immature form, be consumed if adequately disguised. This necessary disguise figures in the clever relation Martial draws between Caecillius, chef of *Lagenaria*, and Atreus, chef of Thyestes' sons:

> Atreus Caecilius cucurbitarum
> Sic illas quasi filios Thyestae
> In partes lacerat secatque mille.

> *Caecilius, the Atreus of Pumpkins,*
> *cuts them, as Atreus did the sons of Thyestes,*
> *into parts and divides them in a thousand ways.* (trans. Greer DuBois)

External Links & Sources

Agriturismomantova.it. http://www.agriturismomantova.it/
Alessandro Cagossi, "History of Pumpkin Tortelli," Seven Fishes Blog, http://www.typepad.com/services/trackback/6a00d8345634d569e2012875d4c1d1970c
"Ancient Humans Brought Bottle Gourds To The Americas From Asia," in *Science Daily*, 12-14-2005. http://www.sciencedaily.com/releases/2005/12/051214081513.htm
Art museums.

Luca Bergamin, "In Mantua, Discovering the Italian Origins and Delicacies of Halloween, in *La Stampa*," 10-20-2011, http://worldcrunch.com/food-travel/in-mantua-discovering-the-italian-origins-and-delicacies-of-halloween-/c6s4016/

Catholicism.

Conversations with family & friends.

Digital Princess, at University of California Humanities Research Institute, http://uchri.org/awardees/residential-research-groups/digital-princess-spring-2013/

Food preparation, home-based.

Gardening.

Gift-giving.

Karen Hursh Graber, "The Pumpkin, An Ancient Mexican Native: La Calabaza Grande" http://www.mexconnect.com/articles/2179-the-pumpkin-an-ancient-mexican-native-la-calabaza-grande

Growing pumpkins and other vine crops in Wisconsin, A guide for fresh-market growers, http://learningstore.uwex.edu/assets/pdfs/a3688.pdf

Imaginative leaps.

Italy.

Janick J, Paris HS (2008), "What the Roman emperor Tiberius grew in his greenhouses," http://www.hort.purdue.edu/newcrop/2_13_Janick.pdf

Janick J, Paris HS (2006) "The cucurbit images (1515–1518) of the Villa Farnesina, Rome," *Annals of Botany* 97: 165-176. http://www.ncbi.nlm.nih.gov/pmc/articles/PMC2803371/

Janick J, Paris HS, Parrish DC (2007) "The cucurbits of Mediterranean antiquity: Identification of taxa from ancient images and descriptions," *Annals of Botany* 100: 1441-1457. http://www.ncbi.nlm.nih.gov/pmc/articles/PMC2759226/

Cynthia Ott, *Pumpkin: The Curious History of an American Icon*, University of Washington Press, 2012. http://www.pumpkincurioushistory.com/cindy-ott.html

Painting.

Parenting.

Poetry.

Recioto, and Tortelli di Zucca, at About.com. Italian Food. http://italianfood.about.com/od/stuffedpasta/r/blr0981.htm

Renaissance historical fiction.

Save Dupree Studios. http://www.savedupreestudios.org/

Shakespeare. *Complete Works.*

Tortelli di zucca | mantova e dintorni, Thursday, December 29th 2011, www.mantovaedintorni.com/tortelli-di-zucca.html

giornate

We need to build economic theory, as well as policies informed by those theories on a more realistic assumption of human nature and human agency—taking "homo-socius" rather than "homo-economicus" as our starting point. Assuming that people are genuinely social provides a more optimistic view of human capacities to build and maintain institutions and to pursue the common good. Mobilizing these human capacities is crucial in order to address the huge and manifold challenges of our time. — Margunn Bjornholt & Ailsa McKay, "Advances in Feminist Economics in Times of Economic Crisis," Bjornholt & McKay (eds.), *Counting on Marilyn Waring: New Advances in Feminist Economics* (2014)

(Sesto. Fog. 12/7/2008)

First time we've lived in walking distance
from an Ikea, just two
miles down the road along the airport runway,
fog too dense
this afternoon to have any sense
of what's a few
feet out in any direction, and though my
husband, who has made the trek already, reassures us

that this slice of Sweden, bright blue and yellow
like September sky, lies, if the mist
would lift, directly ahead at the end
of the path bordered by the empty
field to the right and tall barbed wire fence to the left,
it's a miracle when we finally find the parking lot's edge, its materialized sign.

(Bloomsbury. The Dickens' House. 10/24/2008)

Mid-way through a day
devoted to the British Museum, I tear
my children from their slow pour over
glass-cased collections, absorbed in each display
of ancient archeological minutiae,
which I have watched with less than patient eyes, take an hour's
break to walk to the nearby book-packed, paper-stacked house where
Dickens produced *Nicholas Nickleby*,

that giant tome, at about the same time that Lord Elgin
on war-break in Greece was collecting souvenirs,
loading up a ship of ancient
monuments, procured, the Brits still insist,
to keep those treasures *safe from harm*, stuffing them like gilt-
edged sheets inside this hard-bound edifice.

(Siena. St. Catherine's Head. 9/26/2008)

It all starts after too little
time to look alike, *duomo* to *duomo*, one frescoed
masterpiece and the next covering a chapel's walls and ceilings, floored
one moment, forgot the next. Each cathedral
has its Giotto, its Duccio, its Cimabue, Massacio, Raphael.
Myriad Madonnas, plentiful Peters, surplus Sebastians, armload
of Annunciations, Ascencions, Assumptions, restored
to vivid brilliance or faded invisible, every single

one of which gratifies the viewer, their totality
in my middle-aged mind a mass of ill-defined
edges, blurred shapes, transparence stacked one
on top another so that this Virgin's face bleeds through that Eve's thigh—
why I'm grateful to come upon anything that can stand
on its own—no matter how odd, how grim.

(London. The Tower. 10/16/2008)

A place you never knew you longed to see,
this Norman castle grew by accretion
over centuries, added to by one
ruler then the next, legends growing like the many
towers and walls which make it. We
scramble up each one
on winding stairs that bring us to dead-ends some
times, sometimes into open chambers and tiny

chapels or the Tudor toilet, or the cells
where those who crossed
God's anointed earthly servant
came to grief, graffitied names and messages still cut into walls—
frescos that tell their collective story. We pause a moment
to shudder. Head outside to catch the morning's weak sunlight.

Reliquary of Debt

(Florence. Piazza le Degli Uffizi. 12/14/2008)

They're fixed in my mind's gallery,
those living statues, street performers as permanent
as anything carved out of bone, not
marble, cast in flesh, not bronze, can be, positioned at precisely
regular intervals along the *passagio* between the Arno
and the *Piazza del Signoria*, rivals to the stone-draped
figures of Dante, Giotto, Petrarch at
their backs for silence and immobility.

There's Leonardo—the folds of his heavy white robe falling
about his feet exactly as Bernini might have brought
linen to life; Lorenzo the Magnificent,
gilded to the ends of his eyelashes; Galileo looking
off, a little disappointed, telescope pressed
to the quiet bellows of his caged lungs, his controlled heart.

(Florence. Santa Felicita. 10/8/2008)

It's just another *Imperishable*
Masterpiece, the Pontormo in the dark
corner on the right. You have to stick
change into the metal box if you want the chapel
to give up its light. There's only one, though you can see the hole
hacked through a frescoed companion to make
a door for some later patron. *The Deposition* survives this grave mistake
of art history in all

its glowing glory—testament
to pink, to green, its twisted figures clothed
in spandex body suits, transparent wash
of skin, predicting four hundred years in advance Expressionism.
You want to know what happened
to color in those centuries, but only euro gone, the lights go off.

(Warwick. The Lawn. 10/21/2008)

It's a mistake we're here at all, an accident,
climbing stairs and battlements, racing
around an hour before the connecting train taking
us to Shakespeare's grave: lucky happenstance
that the sun's come out, that
we're here at noon for the firing
of the trebuchet, one-ton rock flung
like a ping pong ball a quarter-mile at

a pop downfield. Though I don't know
at the time, it's the trip's peak
for my 12-year-old. Congenial
enough about museums, cathedrals, abbeys, literary
graves & ruins he's sick of seeing, he takes back
a palm-sized model of this medieval military marvel.

(Pompeii. Porta Nocera. 11/29/2008)

The umbrellas sold at Italy's tourist
sites, railway stations, ancient ruins,
fountains, piazzas, art museums,
shop-lined bridges, crowded markets
by undocumented workers
operating out of baby strollers,
car trunks, palms—low expectations
on all sides—never outlast,

like treaties, the storm for which they're bought—and why should
they?—priced at 4
or 5 euro apiece, pocket change that covers see-through nylon,
resistant enough to water but lacking adequate thread
and time to secure
each vertex to the metal web that turns inside out in the thinnest wind.

Reliquary of Debt

(Rome. Santa Marie en Cosmedin. 11/14/2008)

Just inside the portico of this ancient
church built over Greek
ruins at the Forum's edge grins the pocked
gray Triton face, *Boca de la Veritá*, teeth intact,
through whose oracle mouth visitors insert
a virtue-testing sacrificial wrist. Unwilling to risk
his kiss of truth, its consequence or extra cost, I veer from the line, look
at relics lying under glass instead. *There's Saint*

Valentine's skull, I gasp. The children
resist my attempt to assign
significance to this most unvalentine
like token of a long-moribund
holiday at our house, celebrated back then by cutting
out endless pink hearts, recycled as soon as they looked away—flesh, not bone.

(Sesto. Art History Lecture. 10/7/2008)

Caravaggio's on a pilgrimage
of another kind, running
from Rome, from one town to the next, leaving
as he goes a trail of low-wage
portraits—high/low, old/young—on the edge
of poverty, starvation even, staying
one step ahead of the law and just managing
sometimes to set shutters swinging as the door bursts open, page

on the table half-empty, the paint
wet, the apple still crisp, the boy just pulling
a loose sheet up around his bare white neck—
keeping his supplies together in a leather case
with shoulder strap—no need to learn that lesson twice—everything
ready to move on in a few moments to save his own dark neck.

(Rome. Keats' House. 11/15/2008)

His tiny bedroom window overlooks the *Spanish Steps*,
famous writhing stairs that carry
traffic between discontinuities of topography:
two streets that couldn't otherwise connect,
piazza and fountain below; above, another hilltop prospect
in this sinusoidal city; between high and low,
immigrant vendors wave unending wares: wind-up toys, *roses for the lovely*
lady, cashmere. If you shove your way to the correct

spot between water and stairs and stare, its waves and curves disappear
into an illusion of ruled lines that stack
one on top another like the page of a notebook, the kind
I carry in the backpack I have to check at the top of five winding flights, in order
to squeeze into the hall leading to the blank desk,
the single bed, where Keats arrived, just twenty-five, intending to recover, not to die.

(Bath. The Museum of Fashion. 10/20/2008)

Making our way the length of St. James's Parade, we take—
en route from the elaborate Roman ruin that gives this town
its name to its other major attraction—
a shower, at least get soaked,
our rain coats little palmed paper scraps that do nothing to repel the ink
the sky marks us with, so that we don't even
dare enter the Jane Austen
Center as we walk

past, press on to the Assembly
Rooms, where we shake like three abandoned dogs in the foyer,
pointed wordless to the coat rack, wet to the skin
when we come upon the other patrons stepping into corsets at a three-
paneled mirror,
squealing, these middle-aged women, ignoring our still dripping presence.

(Madison. Monroe St. 8/27/2008)

Up all night pacing past my oldest's
locked door and knocking now and then to check his progress/its lack
as he sorts tall stacks
of books and papers
to leave for college, I manage to focus
on my small role in this last task,
fetching twister seals and plastic garbage sacks
he shoves

away—until he drives away
without a wave, and I'm left
with everything that takes his place,
that fills the empty
room, that sits on the stripped
bed among the heaps of unbagged trash.

(Rome. Villa Borghese. 11/15/2008)

It's the exaggerated twist of the god's tunic
scrolled behind him that's the most
compelling aspect of this Baroque piece, not
the fingers interlaced with twigs and leaves, nor bark
racing up the panic-
faced nymph's bare trunk. *Poor Apollo.* He's almost
there but for the seconds that he must have lost
to the wind dragging on that extravagant torqued

cloth, a clock, whose turning
hands outpace his own stretching
toward Daphne whom he's reached—
as every corkscrew in those tight-winding
folds attests, the whole weighty works pointing
away, away from the moment he leans in to seize—too late.

Reliquary of Debt

[Skype]

Atreus Caecilius cucurbitarum
Sic illas quasi filios Thyestae
In partes lacerat secatque mille.
Gustu protinus has edes in ipso,
Has prima feret alterave cena,
Has cena tibi tertia reponet,
Hinc seras epidipnidas parabit.
Hinc pistor fatuas facit placentas,
Hinc et multiplices struit tabellas
Et notas caryotidas theatris.
Hinc exit varium coco minutal,
Ut lentem positam fabamque credas;
Boletos imitatur et botellos,
Et caudam cybii brevesque maenas.
Hinc cellarius experitur artes,
Ut condat vario vafer sapore
In rutae folium Capelliana.
Sic inplet gabatas paropsidesque
Et leves scutulas cavasque lances.
Hoc lautum vocat, hoc putat venustum,
Unum ponere ferculis tot assem.

[4/25/13 12:02:25 AM] Poet: wow. some of that's vaguely familiar.
[4/25/13 12:02:56 AM] Poet: a lot packed into "atreus of pumpkins"
[4/25/13 12:03:01 AM] Poet: !
[4/25/13 12:03:49 AM] Poet: here's the english snippet I have: You'll eat it [pumpkin] as an appetizer, as a side dish, as a dessert, bland flat cakes, candies of every shape and size, and pastries...
[4/25/13 12:03:59 AM] Poet: "atreus of pumpkins" is SOOOOOOO much better

GiottO : Jesture : Sleights of Hand : Arena Chapel

Justice
takes everyone in:
under her villagers dance,
soldiers hunt, merchants
flourish.

Flourishing
a flower-offering
idol who leads on leash,
Faithless limps/is dragged
to flame.

Flourishing
the creed, Faith squares
off against Idolatry,
clothes ripped, fresh from the
battle.

Flames lick
Envy's skirts, almost
understandably, but Despair?
Harder to judge
smugly.

Battling
her own demons—drink,
gossip, violence—Temperance
watches Wrath a bit
smugly.

Smugly,
perhaps, Charity
and Hope both receive divine
presents, their sisters'
Justice.

August—
I don't mind its mid-
day heat, snore-broke peace, workshop sunk deep in wine-
some sleep.

Sum sleep
failing, he maps grand
chapels in his mind, paints in
each fresh-counted sheep,
gets up.

Some sleep
fills each afternoon:
Don't even think of touching
the painting until
we're up!

Give up
Master: that one's not
real, though I'd have sworn other
wise: you must speak to
the youth.

We're up,
Boy, back to work: I
can't understand how you keep
going round the clock—
ah—youth!

A youth-
ful joke, the fresco
fly: *Get off!* the master yells
flapping. *Shoo! I hate*
August.

Am I
to have no other
design? Gentle joke: *It is*
enough and more than
enough.

Enough.
Send it and see. When
you describe its production,
recognition will
follow.

Enough
joking! I can't take
nothing back to Rome to show
His Holiness. Please.
My job.

Follow
me to Florence? my
master asked, spying my sheep.
Just ten, I said, *Yes,*
I will.

My job
takes me out often.
Dull work, but I can still see
that boy's steady hand,
eye, will.

I will
teach, Cimabue
promised, *painting. I'll finish this*
first. Please. Step out of
my light.

Fake space,
fake light fill two small
choirs, painted where the transept
should extend Giotto's
design.

Designed
so that frescoes not
created could be viewed nights,
two oil lamps dangle
unlit.

Designed
so that it's always
morning, always sunny, light
comes in through one side
only.

Unlit
by any painted
hints to fill in the dim blanks,
viewers must extend
the list.

Only
its marked squares shape
these blanks—couldn't the artist
have laid their outlines
at least?

The list
of chapel traveling
through history increased
but for this present
fake space.

✳

He maps
in his mind, chapels,
no bigger sometimes than wall-fit
niches which still
hold all.

Hold all
of this in your mind
at a glance? Of course you can't—
no one could. Let me
explain.

Hold all
your jokes: simpletons
can't control their witlessness.
Perhaps an evil
devil—

Explain-
ing each story to
his simple son, the father
talks for hours about
Mercy.

Devils
them? But I believe
in mercy—look at Tobit,
look at Lazarus.
Mercy.

Merci-
ful God: to listen
to that man talk through each pane
to a boy whose mind
he maps!

✳

Grieving,
Giotto puts his brush
down to cry at the wall, what's
in his mind, and their
difference.

Different
suns whiten the cut
away houses, cross sections
bright at the front, dark
behind.

Different
light sources brighten
the painting's surface, but not
the night sky, not Anne's
candle.

Behind
again, the workshop
scrambles to finish one more
fresco, stays up through
dark nights.

Candles
never helped—you'd think
they'd have worked through noonday sun,
saved food/sleep for long
dark nights.

Dark nights
of the soul find each
saint—paint shouldn't hide that fact,
sanctified by pain
and grief.

✳

Look, son,
there's Lazarus—white,
unwrapped, overlapped by Christ's
disciples, upstaged
by Christ.

By Christ,
boy, can you picture
the smell when they fished him out?
Great hunk of rotting
flesh, yes?

Flesh, yes,
but more, I paint soul,
paint gesture. Her empty hands,
long look, his sharp turn
to warn.

By Christ,
I wouldn't, dead, want
to come back—and not like that—
bound head to foot, trapped,
gawked at.

Gawked at
by Passover crowds
in death, Christ's return draws one
spurned girl. *Touch me not!*
he warns.

I warn
you once more—do not
come so close. Sorry, but he
can't see otherwise,
my son.

❄

Leasing
looms to weavers, all
business, Giotto fixes rates—
one-hundred-twenty
percent.

Purchas-
ing his father's soul,
Enrico kneels to Mary,
hands her the chapel,
palms out.

Pursing
his lips, the painter
writes: *Lacking in goods means good*
sense will also be
lacking.

Palms out
the artist tallies—
four *giornate* on that face,
credit against his
lending.

Lacking
persuasive power,
Judas wrongly judges he'll
pay back his loan re-
lending.

Lending
each other a hand
into heaven, the two men
determine terms for
leasing.

❄

Sit down—
look at the calm *O*
in the center, at the hole
he's drawn like curtains
in time.

In time,
perhaps, he'll reach through
the world's opening with one
thin hand, offering
it up.

In time
we'll find ourselves split
in two piles—*tortured* and *bored*—
if this vision is
correct.

Then up
they'll crawl, climbing what
they can find: ladders, crosses,
devils, neighbors, all
objects.

Correct
or not, he decides,
there's room here for all, and God,
mellowing, doesn't
object.

Object?
As if I didn't
know it would turn out this way!
But use earphones—keep
it down!

Maybe
in the afterlife
virtue/vice won't vie one version or other for
space, time.

Space, time
erase virtuoso
lines—what's left could mean virtual-
ly anything—verbs
drifting.

Space-time
might allow do-overs:
prove Prudence a version
of Folly or vice-
versa.

Adrift
on flat planes, visual
and moral sleight of hands, not
verb-stone or noun-stroke
convert.

Versa-
tile virgins or not,
vertical, verifia-
ble visions, verging
on verse.

Reversed,
inverted, converse
of every vernacular
verity, adverb-
ing *be*.

A note on the poem: The medieval/renaissance Italian fresco workshop is one of the great examples of situational artistic collaboration driven by meaningful purpose for a real and interested audience, which is not to idealize either the product or the circumstances that created it, but to appreciate the lessons it continues to hold for contemporary arts. This is a selection from a longer piece. I created its form to mimic the Arena (Scrovegni) Chapel and the building blocks of fresco workshops as well as to facilitate a poetry collaboration with Greer DuBois. I wanted the form to capture and imitate the way that individual paintings in a fresco cycle stand on their own but connect with other paintings to create a larger story, sometimes playing off pieces painted above, below, or across from each other. I call the individual, syllabic stanza units used throughout the poem *giottos* after the painter who inspired them. These units fit together architecturally, one beginning with the same two syllables that end its predecessor. Although these *giottos* are built in the round (an "O"), any number of alternative spaces could be created this way. The Os included here often relate to specific paintings in the Arena Chapel (available to view on many websites including Web Gallery of Art wga.hu/frames-e.html?/html/g/giotto/padova/index.html). They also reference stories about Giotto and the chapel as well. Characters and symbols recur along the walls of the Arena Chapel; in contrast to major art museums like the Vatican or the Uffizi where individual pieces are mostly displayed out of context from their original churches, the Arena Chapel presents a story in its totality as it was conceived for a particular space, preserving its grand original narrative and scope. Although the syllabic form with its two-syllable entry/exit points leads to telegraphic statements at the micro level, the smaller pieces can build a larger whole—much as fresco artists would have found this lamb or that face fitting into a grander story. The original project allowed for the production of individual and collaborative work and negotiation between the two. Some other sections of the poem that were created with Greer as well as process notes about our collaboration have been published at the online journals *qarrtsiluni* and *Poemeleon.*

[Skype]

[4/26/13 11:41:02 PM] Poet: I'm trying to understand exactly what Martial would have meant by pumpkin/cucurbita

[4/26/13 11:41:09 PM] Poet: obviously not our pumpkins

[4/26/13 11:41:22 PM] Poet: not the pumpkins of present day italy

[4/26/13 11:41:28 PM] Poet: which are american

[4/26/13 11:41:30 PM] Poet: right

[4/26/13 11:41:42 PM] Poet: and possibly cucumber, possibly melon of some sort

[4/26/13 11:42:22 PM] Poet: one thing I read suggested that he meant Lagenaria seceria, but that is more of a hard gourd

[4/26/13 11:42:38 PM] Poet: so it doesn't make as much sense.

[4/26/13 11:43:08 PM] Poet: if he really means that they're eaten

[4/26/13 11:43:14 PM] Poet: though maybe he doesn't

[4/26/13 11:49:14 PM] Poet: I've read a couple of other articles by those authors

[4/26/13 11:49:23 PM] Poet: but not that one

[4/26/13 11:49:46 PM] Poet: they broke the villa farnesina story…

[4/26/13 11:50:02 PM] Poet: about it having the first illustrations of pumpkins from the   new world

[4/26/13 11:51:48 PM] Poet: those bottle gourds look pretty obscene…

giornate

Countries/cultures go bankrupt all the time. Corporations are by definition bankrupt. But people? Walk away. #Inter(bank)rupt #PoCoPilgrim

(Padua. Stazione Centrale. 9/21/2008)

Sitting on top a wall in the train
yard because the benches, full of tired
Sunday evening travelers, will not yield
space, we wait to return
to Florence from Venice via Padua, where we've seen
the Scrovegni/Arena Chapel, Giotto's masterwork, its quilted
picture bible laid out to visitors for seven hundred
years—the just-restored colors a newly open

pastel box except where the rains came in through the façade,
except where the salt flower blooms on an Apostle's cheek.
But the chapel sky is always blue, bright blue,
and clear, unlike the gray and cloudy vault of the station where we stand
now with our children, eating take-out pizza for dinner, cheaping
it through Europe, (mis)leading the way.

(Greenwich. Royal Observatory. 10/23/2008)

In Greenwich we make a dash
for it up the long hill from a quick
visit to the Maritime Museum and the jacket
Admiral Nelson wore at Trafalgar, bullet hole still fresh
as the day he fell, having saved the British
Empire from Napoleon, to the Observatory that looks
out over the whole world, where west, through a trick
of history more than geometry or geography, still meets east, and red-faced, breath-
    less

visitors queue up to put one foot in each hemisphere,
hands on hips, a bestriding
colossus, and after we're done,
race back to London to catch a train to one of the fifty-some Tudor
residences of Henry VIII, another stop along the snaking
Thames we follow from Westminster and back and on to Hampton.

(Florence. Hotel Cimabue. 10/12/2008)

The scientist I did not spend
my life with sits—two days after Iceland goes
bankrupt—across from me, first time in twenty-five years,
in the lobby of the hotel he's staying
on the way to Pompeii with daughters who are not mine.
The children who are not his
sit next to me, shifting uncomfortably, as he predicts
some coming oil crisis, economic collapse, and how we can

prepare for worldwide
panic and famine. He's planted a garden,
and I wonder if he seriously
thinks a few rows of lettuce would stand
between him and apocalypse, umbrella against a storm
of volcanic rock and molten lava.

Wendy Vardaman

(Pisa. Campo Santo. 11/8/2008)

Here we hear the largest
number of languages per square kilometer,
puzzle on a sunny day in November
over a hundred tourists
similarly posed along a line of sight
between the old city door
past the *duomo* toward its *campanile*, one layer
wrapped in plastic like an art

installation, all hands extended
to the blue-sky air, and it takes a little while
to understand that they haven't come from every corner
of the earth to perform Tai-chi or some ritual to keep the world
from flying to pieces at what must be its center, where all
comers want to create the same illusion—to prop up the tower.

(Florence. Piazza le Degli Uffizi. 12/13/2008)

More jester than the artist
who revived portraiture, invented landscape, juggled
jealous patrons deftly, the dumpy dwarf, surrounded
by colossi of Italy's renaissance,
stands hands on hips, round chest
thrust out, for all the world
as if he did bestride it, indifferent in his curled—
and you'd swear belled—shoes to the ridiculous figure he cuts

alongside Lorenzo the Magnificent or his long, thin, elegant
friend, Dante with his laurel crown,
who, tossed out of Florence, lives his last impoverished
in Ravenna, while this *Giotto*, citizen of every city-state
from Milan to Naples, moves among them, pensioned, admired, surrounded
by citizens of his own only nation, the workshop.

(Between Salisbury and Stonehenge. 10/17/2008)

Having made an obligatory
circle around the ring of smaller-than-I'd-imagined stones, listening
as we walk, black rectangles hanging
from loops about our necks, to audio
included with admission, no
place to stop and linger looking
at the ancient stones, here at the center of nothing,
green pasture unrolled like a table round to meet neatly on this sunny

day, at its selvedges, blue sky, we're herded sheep-
like along a low-roped asphalt path, relieved at its end to take
the bus toward town, get off at the multi-storied
ruins of Old Sarum whose hilltop
site we have to ourselves to stroll, to sit, to break
out sandwiches, to stare blankly chewing at cathedral spires below.

(Meta. The Beach. 11/30/2008)

Because we miss the Paestum train that turns out—
everyone knows that—to be a bus,
and because the sea all up and down the coast closes
for bad weather, just one cruise ship rocking at
the horizon and one small fishing boat
close in, we pace
only partly-cloudy Sunday Sorrento's limoncello streets, pause
for lunch, for coffee, for long stares at

the water, climb the long stairways more
than once, collect shells on the sand
and bits of sponge, revisit
then reject an afternoon at Naples' art museum, an hour
from here by train, reject a bus ride on contorted cliff-side
roads, build castles in fast-flattening tide, fast-waning light.

(Arezzo. Casa Petrarch. 12/5/2008)

Walking Arezzo two wet hours, we pass
Petrarch's, hardly stopping when his door
is locked: it's supposed to open at this hour—
according to the guide book—but doesn't, and no one wants
to linger waiting for the appearance
of some annoyed employee on the other
side just reading a romance novel through the downpour,
nothing poetic, or, having spent last

night up arguing with her shiftless boyfriend—
that spendthrift cheat—catching up on needed
rest, wrestling in her underwater dreams
with bill-collecting mermen turned
out in purple tails, neck-ties, and fresh-trimmed
scales, weighing, while we dash for a train, her options.

(Venice. Circling. 9/20/2008)

We take the wrong turn after the Peggy Guggenheim,
can't remember the street
where our hotel room waits, wander one way and another hoping to get
back by chance. From around the corner, two unleashed dogs come
at us barking, but the owner reigns them in, unlocks his home
before we think to ask for help. I resist
communication, don't speak the language, embarrassed
to begin in English, while my fluent husband won't ask directions,

and while it's tempting to begin one of those blame-
assigning arguments here in this dark Venetian
alley in which neither of us, eyes aging,
can read the names of maze-like streets even if we knew the one we wanted,
we retrace our steps instead at length,
go back to the origin of our aimless wandering.

(Sesto. Nightmare. 11/24/2008)

I can just see Dante on his Grand
Tour of the Afterlife, probably
one of a huge group he leaves out of the story
to make himself seem more significant, wearing the little head
set on a color-coded lanyard
and trying to keep up as Virgil, out front with the umbrella,
pushes on, speaking Italian with a heavy
Latin accent, mixing a few historical facts with enough sordid

details to keep everyone interested, moving
quickly through the arty parts and displaying just enough useless
papal trivia to convince
everyone that they couldn't get through Hell without his mediation,
as Dante, jockeying for the best view on the boat, tosses
out quips and epigrams to his tired secretary, no Beatrice.

Reliquary of Debt

(Lucca. San Frediano. 9/13/2008)

She lies in state, princess under glass,
crown of flowers circling her withered head—
those soft white shapes emerging from a blackened
form that by now must feel like granite to the touch,
sharp edges of its rock face
jutting out among petals that do little to hide
the mummified Saint Zita, dead
800 years, her body retrieved two centuries

after burial *miraculously in tact* and since
that displayed to pilgrims, tourists, supplicants.
Saint Zita while she lived smuggled bread
to the poor. Told her father that flowers, not food,
lay hidden in her cloak—*truth*
when uttered by her incorruptible mouth.

(Rome. The Forum. 11/15/2008)

Sy prays to Jupiter
after my husband's rosary chases away
a line of towering clouds, and we
arrive to a Rome whose black noon air
and atmosphere
crackle with the syncretic thunder bolts of these two
competing for every
one's gaze—our god lights up the sky over

St. Peter's, while Sy's hurls lightning
at our guide, misses her by inches,
which is why their group misses the rendezvous,
watches rain pour through the open O of the pantheon
instead, while ours dodges the worst of it outside under arches
and awnings, admiring a rainbow that reconnects the Tiber-divided city.

(Madison. Monroe St. 12/23/2008)

Everyone's back, and we watch, snow
piles mounting higher against our disappearing
yellow house, *The Darjeeling*
Limited entirely by accident, a movie
about pilgrimage, travel, control, letting go
of your luggage, planning
the meaningful journey, parenting & its limits, service, staying
in touch while going your separate ways, how

life can simultaneously be random
and ordered for whatever reason: our option—despite
or maybe because of the fact that we'll all
get smashed and broken
against, when the guideline breaks, a swollen river's sharp-faced
rocks—to choose, whenever we like, to drop everything, to dive into the unknow-
able.

(Sesto. Running Route. 4/week)

The streets of Sesto after a week
in Rome have widened,
emptied, straightened,
as threatening as a stray cloud's sunwink,
an arch-backed
cat, a language that I do not understand.
There is the shuffler, who yelled
at us as we ran past *to walk*,

and the last black-clad, cane-carrying pair
of old ladies in the country, arms linked,
returning from market and mass,
who do not shrink or retreat but force us into the street where the wheel-chair
bound man, keeper looking
askance, calls and waves, *Ciao mama*, *Ciao figlia*, and we wave back.

[Skype]

[4/29/13 12:57:31 PM] Poet: thanks again for your Latin help …

[4/29/13 12:57:58 PM] Poet: I changed the epigraph because of that to the Atreus part, which was better than what I originally had

[4/29/13 12:58:12 PM] Poet: that Annals of Botany article was also really helpful

[4/29/13 12:58:32 PM] Poet: so this version is down from 7 sonnets

[4/29/13 12:58:46 PM] Poet: because I needed to only have 1 page for the gift poem

[4/29/13 12:58:48 PM] Poet: aargh

[4/29/13 12:59:12 PM] Poet: left out a ton of stuff--I'd thought about just doing one sonnet, but felt like I wanted more

[4/29/13 12:59:35 PM] Poet: so this reads a little more Marianne Moore than I'd like, but that's the way it goes

[4/29/13 1:01:06 PM] Poet: it's roughly 20 syllables/line

[4/29/13 1:01:24 PM] Poet: though I had a hard time counting Italian "syllable" since they're so flexible

[4/29/13 1:01:58 PM] Poet: I don't know--does it make sense or seem too book reporty?

[4/29/13 1:03:41 PM] Poet: I feel like I've cooked down 1000 lbs of watery pumpkin to a cupful …

[4/29/13 1:04:09 PM] Poet: there's at least 20 sources in their …

[4/29/13 1:04:11 PM] Poet: there

[4/29/13 1:04:29 PM] Poet: probably more, plus some significant flights of research fancy/insanity

20149847R00060

Made in the USA
San Bernardino, CA
29 March 2015